T0128981

The
FUNctional
Facilitator

Because Attitude Is Everything!

Jeanne Taylor McClellan
and Debbi Fuhrer

iUniverse, Inc.
Bloomington

The FUNctional Facilitator
Because Attitude Is Everything

iUniverse books may be ordered through booksellers or by contacting:

iUniverse
1663 Liberty Drive
Bloomington, IN 47403
www.iuniverse.com
1-800-Authors (1-800-288-4677)

ISBN: 978-1-4620-6965-1 (sc)
ISBN: 978-1-4620-6967-5 (hc)
ISBN: 978-1-4620-6966-8 (e)

Printed in the United States of America

iUniverse rev. date: 12/19/2011

Contents

About the Authors

Jeanne is an intelligent, witty, ambitious, and laid back business owner. Her facilitation style is informal and encourages all group members to express themselves and participate in discussions.  When needed, Jeanne isn't afraid to stir the pot and ask the difficult questions to start crucial discussions–especially when there's a big elephant in the room that no one wants to address.

If Jeanne had to choose between organizing her desk and thinking about the big picture of a project, she would pick the big picture without a second thought. Jeanne uses this strength of seeing the big picture when facilitating groups and helps others to share in the vision. Those who have experienced Jeanne's coaching and facilitating know that she has a genuine interest in helping people become the leaders they are capable of being.

Debbi is an intelligent, hard-working, detailed-oriented student of human behavior. Her facilitation style is calm and accepting of individual differences in communication. Debbi has no difficulty in clarifying groups' objectives and directing them to move forward toward achieving their objectives.

If Debbi had to choose between creating the vision and outlining the details of a project, she would outline those details without a second thought. Debbi uses this strength to keep the project on track and the participants on task. Those who have experienced Debbi's organizational skills and facilitation prowess know that she has a genuine interest in helping people reach their specific goals in an open and honest atmosphere.

And for those of you looking for our credentials...

Jeanne Taylor McClellan has a BS in Education and an MS in Adult Counseling with certifications in Business Coaching and Forensic Psychology. She has been working in Organizational Development for more years than most of you readers have been alive!

Debbi Fuhrer has a BA in International Relations, an MS in International Marketing, and is currently pursuing her Masters in Health Administration. She has been facilitating groups within educational and healthcare facilities for more than 10 years.

Jeanne and Debbi co-facilitate workshops on FUNctional Facilitating. You don't want to miss these workshops. You'll experience two very different facilitators as you learn why *attitude is everything!*

Preface

The dictionary definition of facilitation is "to make something easy" so why not make it easy on you, the Facilitator? This book is intended to give you an introduction to facilitation with an approach that is light, but focused, as we dive into the basics of facilitation and give tips on how to be effective. We've included resources you can access to increase your personal facilitation skills, as well as some real stories to illustrate the basics of facilitation.

Facilitators are not born; they are made after much learning and practicing. In fact, the success of any Facilitator is dependent entirely upon the confidence and trust that the group has in him or her. That confidence and trust develops when the group experiences a Facilitator who understands and uses the basic elements of F.A.C.I.L.I.T.A.T.I.N.G.

You'll notice that each chapter focuses on an important facilitating topic. We've made each chapter a standalone topic so you can refer to the topics when they are most relevant to your facilitating experiences. We've included a real story related to each topic, some basic information and suggestions, the FUN part of this topic, and attitudes a good Facilitator needs to handle that topic.

Everyone has his or her own facilitation style, including the two of us. You'll probably notice that the chapters have different writing styles; that's because not only do we have different facilitating styles, but we also have different personalities and approaches to telling stories.

We decided to write this book together because we've had numerous experiences facilitating groups- some good, some bad, and some very ugly. We wanted to share these stories because from each one of those experiences, we have become better Facilitators ourselves. As you dive into facilitation, you'll develop your own facilitation style, which is just one of the FUN parts of being a Facilitator.

For you, this book may be just the beginning. There is much more to learn so please refer to the back pages for a list of additional resources.

Acknowledgments

We'd like to thank Cher Shipman for the wonderful illustrations, which truly brought our words and stories to life. You were very patient through the brainstorming stages and came back with images of what our words really looked like!

We'd also like to thank Jessica Shapiro for helping with the initial edits of this book. While we originally went into shock after seeing all of your red comments, we concede that the book is now much better as a result of your detailed revisions!

F = FRAMING

The workshop was advertised as "essential to our personal and professional growth," a place where we would learn presentation techniques that would make us stand out from the rest and have people lining up to hear us speak. The speaker was described as "dynamic, exciting, and entertaining." The location was a lovely hotel in a beautiful area. Three days in such a place learning new skills with an expert was an event not to be missed!

On the first morning, all the participants met in the hotel restaurant. The excitement was palpable. We walked as a group to the meeting room, signed in, put on our nametags, and entered the room.

The room was large with lots of open space. At the front of the room a small platform held a podium and flipchart. A row of ten folding chairs had been placed directly in front of the platform allowing only twelve inches between the knees of the occupants and the front of the platform. Three more rows with ten chairs each had been placed closely behind that first row. There were mere inches between each chair and minimal leg space between each row.

We were directed to take a seat and get comfortable —
difficult to do when you are literally shoulder to shoulder with the stranger next to you and your knees are pressing into the back of the person sitting in front of you. After what seemed to be a long time, the presenter bounded to the platform to loud, high-energy

music. He greeted us with extreme, boisterous enthusiasm which was overwhelming and out of place for a group of thirty-three professionals.

As the day progressed fewer people returned after each break and the cluster of chairs got tighter. (The presenter's staff actually removed the empty chairs so we were always sitting close together). Despite the size of the room, the atmosphere was suffocating. We did ask why we were seated so closely in such a large space. The presenter replied, "This way we get to really know each other and lose our boundaries."

What was lost was more than half of the original group by day's end. Needless to say, the atmosphere in the room stifled any possibility of professional growth.

Framing the atmosphere in which any facilitation is to take place is essential to the success of the experience. There are two parts to this frame: basic physical logistics and specific goal setting.

Basic Physical Logistics

This includes seating arrangements, lighting, temperature, and sound quality. Overall, it is important to keep participants comfortable. Rooms that are too hot or too cold, lighting that is too bright or too soft, and sound systems that crackle undermine participants' ability to pay attention to the work. Test all of these things before the session to ensure that the group will be focused and ready to contribute.

Different arrangements of chairs and tables in the room will give you different results with the group. A strong Facilitator manages the group subtly and seating arrangements will add or subtract from that subtlety.

Classroom Style - Arranging the chairs or tables one behind the other in rows puts the Facilitator in the front of the room and makes her the center of attention. However, this arrangement may remind some people unpleasantly of the classrooms of their youth.

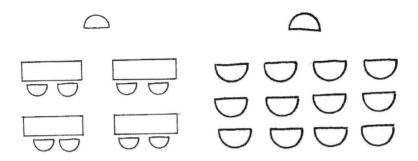

U Shaped – The open setup facilitates discussion and lets the Facilitator walk among the group. To avoid having your back to any of the participants for any length of time it is important to move around the room with this setup.

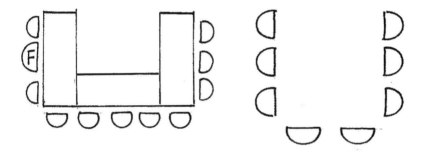

Board Room – Here someone sits at the head of the table. This arrangement is best when it is necessary to create a hierarchy. This style may limit interaction among the group as side-by-side seating may interfere with open communication within the group.

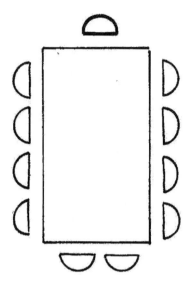

Goal Setting

After the group members are physically comfortable you are then able to get them comfortable with the task at hand. Facilitating a group is a journey, and, just as in any journey, it is vital to know where you are going.

Each participant must be able to articulate the group's goals. The goals must be **S.M.A.R.T.**: **S**pecific, **M**easurable, **A**ttainable, **R**ealistic, and **T**imely. It is the job of the Facilitator to lead the group to these goals.

Once everyone agrees to the goals, the next decision is how the group will measure the outcome of its work. That measurement determines whether the group is succeeding in its work. Ask: "How will the group be different when the session is over?" and "What has the group accomplished specifically?"

With these questions answered, the group is ready to move forward with its project.

Use this framing process for every meeting with the group. Always check the logistics and then revisit the goals and measurements. This provides consistency and keeps the group on track.

The FUN of Framing is...

Watching the participants interact exactly as you wanted because of the atmosphere you created with proper framing.

Your FUNctional Attitude Focuses on:

- **Organization** to enable you to visualize the process as you set up the room.

- **Flexibility** to prepare you to handle the unexpected with a sense of humor.

A = ASSESSING

The project had been assigned four weeks earlier. The participants had been handpicked by the CEO based on their expertise. The Facilitator's responsibility was to bring all these minds together and keep them moving forward to get the project done on time and under budget.

The Facilitator had prepared himself for this group. Before meeting the group, he had assigned each team member to take the Myers-Briggs Type Indicator (MBTI) online. He had reviewed and analyzed the results of the individual inventories and had reviewed the list of participants, their job responsibilities, and their various departments.

Attendees trickled into the room, coffee in hand, ready to work.

John and George were both new to the company, experts on the subject matter, and specifically hired for this project. Both were ready to work, but neither man knew anyone in the room.

The Facilitator lingered at the front of the room. As people entered, he smiled, nodded at some, made brief eye contact with others, and generally observed individual and group behavior. He watched as people formed distinct groups, saving spaces for others who had not yet arrived.

He noticed John and George surveying the room deciding where to sit. He knew that George would find a group, introduce himself, and join them. He knew that John would find an empty table and sit away from the rest of the group.

Combining the information from the MBTI with the background studies he had done on each participant enabled him to guide the group effectively to complete the project. More importantly, he was confident in his ability to adjust his facilitating style and get everyone focused and functioning.

As with any project, the more information you have before you start, the better prepared you are to do the work. Make no mistake: facilitation requires work before, during, and after the actual connection. So let's take this in steps.

Step 1 – Know Your Group

The more you know about each individual in the group the better equipped you are to manage the whole group. The Myers-Briggs Type Indicator is just one of the many inventories you could use. Also, the more each participant knows about his personal style of communication the more prepared he will be to participate in the group.

Pay attention to each participant's body language and speaking styles. Encouraging them to share information about their job responsibilities or just asking how their day has been will help you to assess the attitude of each individual and the mood of the group as a whole.

Step 2 – Prepare for the Unexpected

When you prepare for facilitation, take some time to envision some of the situations that could arise. Choose the ones that could be the most challenging for you, and plan for those with enough detail that you will be able to adjust your style seamlessly. The more experience you gather as a Facilitator, the more alternate plans you will have at your disposal to let you smoothly adjust to any situation.

Step 3 – Close the Session

It's important to bring closure to any group. Do this by circling back to the beginning of the session. Ask the group three summary questions:

- **What?**
  What really happened today? Have group members summarize the day from their perspectives.

- **So What?**
  How did today's events fit into the bigger picture? What value did this session bring to the project and to the contribution the group is making?

- **Now what?**
  Where does the group want to go from here? What are its next steps? How will the group move forward?

This is the time for you to be still and let group members discover what they have learned. You may find it difficult to be silent during this time. At most, summarize their learning for them when they are finished and set them up for the next session. Remember that this is their process and that you have ben privileged to share it with them.

The FUN of Assessing is...

Knowing how each person's behavior will unfold as you place them in a new situation – it's almost like being psychic.

Your FUNctional Attitude Focuses on:

- **Preparation** to identify the individual behaviors and uncover the dynamics of the group as a whole.

- **Appreciation** of individual differences and an ability to blend those differences into a cohesive unit

C = COACHING

The team was struggling. Individually they worked well, but when required to work as a team, they fell apart. They constantly bickered among themselves, blaming each other for their poor performance. And, of course, there was a project that had to be completed on time, under budget, and with excellence. The manager called in a Facilitator to get them to pull together.

The Facilitator met with each person individually to get input on the situation. Each person blamed someone else for the problem. Communication was poor and trust was nonexistent. The idea of working together as a team was laughable for this group.

The Facilitator began by recognizing the special skills each individual brought to the group and assigning each a section of the project within his or her skill set. At the next team meeting, everyone reported on his or her progress. The Facilitator thanked each presenter and explained how that section fit into the whole project like a puzzle coming together.

As the visual of the project took shape, the group saw how they were all connected to each other. The simple act of listening to each person's concerns individually, assigning work based on individual skills, and thanking them publicly changed the atmosphere from adversarial to cooperative. Group members still had a long way to go and they had moved forward in their efforts to be a team.

In the remaining meetings, the Facilitator directed and celebrated the group's efforts. He made time to speak one-on-one with individuals who still needed support and encouraged the group as a whole as collaboration increased.

Sports coaches keep their teams focused on the goal. In the same way, you, as a Facilitator, will use coaching techniques to increase your group members' awareness of their purpose and keep them moving forward. You will provide them with techniques to increase their individual and collective learning and you will have each member practice those skills in the group setting. In the coaching role you need to ask the right questions at the right time so you need to be alert to the group's mood and momentum.

Begin coaching the group from the very beginning. It is your responsibility to create a safe environment in which the group will interact. You enhance that safe environment by clarifying the group's goal and processes using exceptional active listening skills. Purposefully pay attention to each individual as they contribute to the discussion. Listen intently. Repeat elements of the discussion so group members may clarify their original input and understanding. Encourage the group members to explore all possibilities and to appreciate the processes they all use to reach the group's goals. At the same time, hold the group and the individuals accountable. And most importantly, celebrate the group's successes.

When the group first forms you may ask:

- What challenges are you facing with this task?

- Have you met this type of challenge before?

- How much time do you have to accomplish this?

You then can serve as a resource for the group. To do this effectively, you must do your due diligence on the topic. You don't need to be the subject-matter expert. However, you do need at least a cursory understanding of the topic.

Remember that your job is not to do the work for the group. Your job is to encourage and support its efforts as it moves forward. That requires you to pay attention to where the group is at the moment and recognize the group's readiness to achieve the goals. At times you may need to be directive and at other times permissive as the group tries things independently. Keeping group members focused on the goal, proud of the work they do, and aware of the value that each person brings to the group is the best way to coach the group to success.

The FUN of Coaching is…

Sharing in an individual's journey to personal and professional development.

Your FUNctional Attitude Focuses on:

- **Intelligence** on both emotional and technical levels.

- **Interest** in the group individually and collectively.

- **Flexibility** to prepare you to steer the group in a different direction when the members go off track.

I = INTERPRETING

A department was working on a promotion program which would be based on level of education and amount of experience. Every month the department met as a whole to decide on the framework for the program, including criteria for advancement, duties, and responsibilities of each level and the selection process. Leading this group was a new director of this department, and he struggled with the different personalities within the department.

When less experienced or more passive members expressed themselves during discussions, a more dominating member would interject, "I think what you mean to say is..." and would change the meaning of the other person's thought to make sure it was aligned with her own agenda. Soon, the other members of the group were hesitant to say anything in the meetings, and the director felt they were at an impasse. In addition, members who didn't feel comfortable speaking during the meeting would come to the director afterwards with their opinions or suggestions, which took a good deal of his time.

The director decided to change the discussion format. He sent out an agenda and a list of questions the group would address, giving the members ample time to prepare their thoughts. At the next meeting, the director went around the table to hear what each person had to say. He made sure the dominating member gave her feedback last. While she wasn't able to give her feedback throughout the meeting, she expressed herself with her body language by crossing her arms, rolling her eyes, and tapping her foot. However, because the other members were prepared for the questions and everyone was given a chance to speak, they voiced their own suggestions and ideas. As different opinions and perspectives were expressed, members grew more confident in their suggestions because the dominating member was not interjecting.

This new format created a more open communication between the members, and they were able to move the project forward. The director also found that this method resulted in fewer "meetings after the meetings."

As the Facilitator, you need to look beyond what is actually being said during the meeting. Look for nonverbal cues. Remember that 93% of all communication is nonverbal, just as the group member exhibited in the above story. Even though she wasn't verbally giving her feedback, any member who looked at her would know exactly how she was feeling about the topic. Observe the nonverbal cues and help each participant feel safe and comfortable expressing himself in the group. Some common nonverbal cues are easily recognized and those exhibiting them often respond to simple techniques.

The Non-Participating Group Member

Often this member will be quiet during the meeting, provide little to no verbal feedback, present with a flat affect during the meeting, and come late to meetings. Try to engage the individual by making her a "Timekeeper." This forces her to stay engaged in the discussion and gives her a purpose of keeping the group on track with the agenda.

You can also engage this member by acknowledging her area of expertise. For example, "Tara, I know that you work with computers on a daily basis, so maybe you have a suggestion on what we can do about this IT problem." This validates her expertise, and encourages her to talk about something that is in her comfort zone.

If the group is brainstorming, try having everyone write down ideas, then go around the room and have everyone share one of his or her ideas. This helps the introverts and quiet participants contribute ideas and opinions.

As in the above story, sometimes these non-participating members come to the Facilitator after the meeting to express themselves. During these "meetings after meetings," encourage the person to voice her thought during the actual meeting so everyone can hear it. You can also ask the member what is preventing her from voicing this in front of the group. This might help determine if there is something you can do to make the member feel more comfortable in the group.

The Dominating Group Member

Acknowledge the member's contribution by paraphrasing what they've said. If it's an idea, record it on newsprint so everyone can see it. Ask "Are there any other suggestions?" or "Does anyone else have something to add?" If the dominant member continues to revisit the topic or idea she has come up with, remind her "We've already put it on the list, and at the moment, we are looking for other ideas."

If this is not a brainstorming session, and the member continues to revisit the same theme repeatedly, suggest that the topic be set-aside for the moment placing it on the Parking Lot★ list to be revisited another time. That way the individual is validated and her idea is recorded, and it does not get the group off track. You can also handle the situation as the Facilitator did in the above story: ask the members to prepare for the discussion prior to the meeting, and then go around the room one by one, leaving the dominant member last. Just make sure that you encourage members to not respond to others' ideas or suggestions until everyone has had a chance to express his or her thought.

The Passive-Aggressive Group Member

Common behaviors for this type of group member may include coming to meetings late, using sarcasm during the meeting, making faces, or not verbally expressing thoughts or ideas during the meeting but emailing the Facilitator after the meeting.

During the meeting, try to engage the participant by asking if she has any thoughts. If you know she has specific knowledge of the topic you are discussing, acknowledge that expertise and create a safe place for her to share her thoughts. If she comes to you after the meeting, validate her thoughts and suggestions and encourage her to share with the rest of the group during the meeting. For instance, say, "Don't be afraid to say what you really think."

The Know-It-All Group Member

This group member is often quick to blame others if something goes wrong, has low tolerance for contradiction, and does not have patience for long drawn-out explanations, preferring bullet points. One suggestion for dealing with this type of group member is to respect and acknowledge that the person perceives herself as an expert. Thank the member for her participation, and ask if anyone else has something to share. In this way, you are validating the information and contribution from this group member, and you are inviting other people to voice their thoughts as well. If the "Know-It-All" continues to bring up the same topics repeatedly, suggest putting the topic in a "Parking Lot" list for another time.

The FUN of Interpreting is...

Learning how to manage individuals so they come together in a group and work as a whole.

Your FUNctional Attitude Focuses on:

- **Awareness** of group members' behaviors and the group's dynamics.

- **Observation** of how members are reacting to the discussion and managing their behaviors.

★ A **Parking Lot** refers to a white board or newsprint pad where you can maintain an ongoing list of questions or issues the group wishes to address.

L = LEADING

A volunteer organization had a diverse group of members and a leader who didn't have control of the group. When the group first started, the leader presented the organization's expectations for its members such as volunteering a certain number of hours, being professional, and showing up on time. The group agreed to complete weekly activities and after each activity the group evaluated its performance by determining the positives of that activity and the "even better if's" so it could improve each time.

Because there was such diversity among the group members there were also different levels of commitment and interest in improving performance from activity to activity. As time went on, certain group members who did not take the evaluation process seriously caused disruption. Instead of bringing the group back on track, the leader let those dominant personalities take control of the group and eventually the evaluation exercise was abandoned.

This lack of control only increased as time went on and soon the dominant personalities infected the entire group with their negativity, their lack of commitment to projects, and unwillingness to put in a lot of work. The leader was passive-aggressive, and, instead of standing up to these members, she simply gave more work to those she knew would not give her a hard time. The group became divided, and tension between members was palpable.

However, the leader did not want to stand up and hold members to the organization's expectations, and she was unable to keep the group together. Ultimately, the group disbanded because of the lack of leadership.

No matter your personality style, you can lead a group. Facilitators are not born; they are created with hard work. While there are some personality types that are more natural leaders than others, anyone can learn the skills to lead a productive meeting. Here are some things to keep in mind:

Know Your Strengths and Your Weaknesses

If you are an extrovert, be aware that you will need to allow members to express their thoughts before you put your own two cents in. If you are an introvert, as the leader in the above story was, know that it might be difficult to address conflicts or derailing conversations.

Know Your Leading Style

While there are different leading styles, one of the main things to remember as a Facilitator is to make sure that your own agenda does not impede the group's progress. You must remain neutral and allow the group to define its own agenda.

Know the Group Members' Expectations

Knowing the purpose of the group will help you provide direction and leadership as the group moves forward. Set meeting guidelines during the first meeting and make sure everyone agrees to them. These guidelines will hold participants accountable to stay on track and be respectful of group members and their ideas. Revisit the purpose of the group often so everyone is on the same page. Be aware that if circumstances change within an organization the purpose of the group may change as well.

By revisiting the purpose and goals of the group, you can manage the expectations of the participants and lead the group to success.

Recognize Group Members' Limits

Like an orchestra conductor, you need to recognize the talents and limitations of the members of your group. Not all members are going to be willing to speak their minds during the first few meetings. However, one of your jobs as Facilitator is to lead the group and create a safe space so members feel comfortable speaking up and expressing their ideas.

Problem Solving and Solutions

When the group needs solutions to a problem, project, or issue, Facilitators need to remain objective and detached from the group to promote full group member participation. Here are a few methods that encourage everyone to share his or her thoughts.

Brainstorming
- Allow time for all group members to call out their ideas.

- Write down all of these ideas on newsprint or on a whiteboard so everyone can read the ideas, or designate a group member to do so.

- While the ideas are being called out, refrain from commenting or reacting; this is just the recording time.

  This method is effective for getting a lot of ideas out to the group. However, if only dominant members are expressing their ideas, try going around the room individually so each person has the opportunity to give input.

Round Table Brainstorming
- Allot five minutes for members to write down their ideas for the current topic.

- Go around the room and have each person call out one idea from his list.

- Write down all ideas on the board so everyone can read them. Again while the ideas are being called out, refrain from commenting or reacting to the ideas.

- Continue going around the room until all ideas have been recorded.

- Read the items on the list for confirmation that all ideas were recorded correctly. You can ask for clarification of ideas so everyone understands each suggestion.

  This method allows for a lot of ideas to be presented to the group; introverted members do better when they have a chance to think their answers through.

Emailing Ideas

- Ask members to vote for specific ideas or send you ideas prior to the meeting.

  This is particularly helpful if there is limited time for discussion during the meeting. You can come to the meeting with a list already compiled and ready to be discussed.

Using these methods of encouraging members to share their ideas requires you to allow time for discussion of ideas, voting, and, ultimately, making a decision. There are a number of ways to lead your group in voting as well.

Individual Voting

- Go around the room and have each person vote for a specific suggestion while you record the results.

- Again, don't make any comments or react to the votes.

  This transparent way of voting could be intimidating for members who are less vocal or are easily influenced by more dominant members.

Silent Voting

- Members are asked to write down their top choice or choices and hand their votes to the Facilitator, who again records the results.

  This allows everyone to have an equal voice. However, it may take more time during the meeting. This could also be done via email as long as members understand that their votes will not be anonymous to the Facilitator.

The FUN of Leading is...

Bringing out the strengths and talents of each group member so that the entire team is the strongest it can be.

Your FUNctional Attitude Focuses on:

- **Management** of the group's time and working with group members to achieve the anticipated outcomes.

- **Confidence** in managing the group.

- **Acknowledgment** of the talents and limitations of the members.

I = INTERACTING

In a Children's Hospital, a Family Advisory Council was made up of parents of pediatric patients, doctors, nurses, support staff, and the hospital administrator. The purpose of the group was to get the families' input on how to improve the services and programs the hospital provides. Because there was such diversity in the group the Facilitator felt it was important to make sure families were comfortable speaking up and voicing their opinions.

Before the group started, the Facilitator emailed members of the group a membership list with names, contact information, and position at the hospital. At the first meeting, each member picked up a printed placard with his or her name on it so everyone could easily call each other by name.

To open the meeting, the Facilitator asked each member to introduce themselves and explain why he or she is part of the group. The family members expressed how grateful they were to have a chance to "give back" after the hospital helped their child and family. The hospital staff members wanted to be part of the group because it reminded them why they do their work at the hospital.

This part of the meeting created bonds between members and allowed the family members to feel safe and encouraged to speak their minds. Family members were pleasantly surprised that they *were able to voice their opinion in front of hospital staff and really felt like they were being listened to. This spoke volumes of the commitment of each group member to continue this honest and sharing environment.*

One of the many roles a Facilitator has is to help group participants to interact with each other in a respectful and productive way.

Preparing the Group

Fostering a productive group often starts even before the meetings begin. As the story suggests, before your group meets for the first time, it is often helpful to send out a list of all group members, their contact information, and their position so it is clear why they are part of the group. If the reason for each person's inclusion is not clear, consider creating short bios so people are familiar with names and positions before meetings begin.

Inspiring Accountability

Acknowledge that meetings take a lot of time and often create work for group members who will need to follow through on projects and assignments. To ensure productive meetings, ask group members to prepare for each meeting. Send out discussion topics or questions ahead of time for members to ponder. This will help introverted personalities who prefer to take some time to think about questions instead of being put on the spot at meetings. Ask group members to make a commitment to read the minutes ahead of time so the group isn't wasting meeting time looking over them. At the end of a meeting, summarize the "asks" of the group members, as well as the deadlines so there is no question what should be accomplished before the next meeting.

Fostering Open Communication

When a group is first meeting, try doing an ice breaker. Some people detest icebreakers, but they often help members bond with each other. Ask each member to tell the group his or her name, what they would like to be called, their position, why they are part of the group, and an interesting fact about themselves at the first meeting. Asking members to give their full name along with what they would like to be called gives them a chance to leave their titles at the door. In the case of the above story, the group included family members as well as medical staff. In most cases, those members who are doctors first introduce themselves with their full title, and then give the group permission to call them by their first name, leveling the playing field.

The FUN of Interacting is...

Witnessing open and honest communication that drives the group forward.

Your FUNctional Attitude Focuses on:

- **Interaction** with the group.

- **Listening skills** to lead the group directly yet subtly.

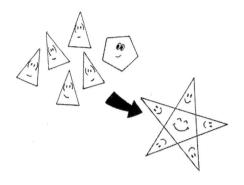

T = TEAMING

The Facilitator was a great guy, friendly and gregarious with a good sense of humor. It was obvious that he was a "people person." He liked people, and he wanted them to like him.

He started each session with a joke. During the session he was quick to insert comic relief into every topic. He closed with a positive sendoff. Usually the group lingered afterwards to continue its camaraderie.

Group members thought of themselves as a team. They socialized after work and on weekends. Most team members accepted the Facilitator as just another member of the team and included him in their social activities.

However, some appeared uncomfortable with his approach and tended to distance themselves from him both in team sessions and social settings. At times, the team as a whole felt unbalanced as the Facilitator switched from facilitating the group to interacting as a teammate. The work was getting done yet something was not quite "right."

As the Facilitator, you walk a fine line between facilitating the group's process and participating as a group member. Both positions are necessary for the development of the group, and a FUNctional Facilitator is able to switch seamlessly between them. Finding your balance between these two roles requires practice and mastery of three major components: trust, shared leadership, and cooperation and collaboration.

Trust

Establishing and maintaining trust is a continuous process. It begins with your very first encounter with the group.

You know "you only have one chance to make a first impression." That first impression establishes your place in the group. At the moment you introduce yourself to the group, each person forms his opinion of you. It is on that opinion that your trust is built.

So how do you make the best impression? Use all of your active listening skills especially those that demonstrate respect of the group as a whole. Listen with concern, empathy, and interest. Paraphrase dialogue for clarity. Ask open-ended questions to encourage individuals in the group to expand on their input. And, most importantly, listen to the group's verbal interactions, and be aware of members' non-verbal communication. Remember, you have the privilege of being part of the group's experience as well as the responsibility to lead group and individual development.

Shared Leadership

All groups have formal leaders and informal leaders. Although these individuals may be very adept at leading, you were brought in to "make things easier." Making things easier for the group includes actively leading it and also teaching group members to lead. You do that by both teaching and modeling appropriate leadership skills.

Cooperation and Collaboration

Every group needs a contract for cooperation and collaboration among all members. As a group begins its work, it is vital for group members to function by "ground rules" they have written by themselves, for themselves. One of the best tools available is the Full Value Contract used by Adventure Based Counseling Group. The Full Value Contract is a living document that describes the group's agreed-upon process for working as a team. Remember, this is the group's contract you will need to enforce as the group goes through its stages of development.

As you walk that line between leader and group member you need to appreciate that the group is going through a balancing act as well. Every group will travel through specific stages of development. In 1965 Bruce Tuckman proposed a four-stage model of group development: **Forming, Storming, Norming, and Performing.** Tuckman said these phases are all necessary and inevitable as a group faces up to challenges, tackles problems, finds solutions, plans work, and delivers results.

You need to understand how each stage develops and segues into the next. And be aware that these stages are circular; any change to the composition of the group will initiate a new circle of development.

The FUN of Teaming is …

Staying aware of the group's progress through these stages and anticipating the shift in progress while you balance between leading and participating.

Your FUNctional Attitude Focuses on:

- **Balance** as you demonstrate appropriate team member behavior while you facilitate the process

A = ARBITRATING

A Facilitator worked with two departments who interacted with each other on the same project, and who were consistently competing against each other. A meeting was requested to come up with a solution to improve communication between the two departments.

Knowing that there was animosity between the two departments and that this would be an emotion-filled meeting, the Facilitator wanted to set the right tone. She emailed all members prior to the meeting to state the purpose of the meeting and request that each person come with suggestions for collaboration and communication between the two departments and plan to share them at the meeting, giving the group a focus with achievable objectives.

To start the meeting the Facilitator acknowledged the tension in the room and commended the departments for wanting to create a better way of communicating. She also acknowledged that each department ultimately wanted to achieve the same goal and to provide the best possible service to customers, to which the entire group agreed. She went over some basic ground rules and informed the group that if the discussion got personal or too adversarial she *would stop the discussion and bring it back to the objectives at hand. All participants agreed to these expectations.*

After the ground rules were set, each participant got a turn to express a suggestion for collaboration with the other department. Someone recorded each idea on a whiteboard, and everyone added suggestions until all ideas were on the board. The Facilitator asked the members to choose one idea the group could agree to work on together. The group came to a consensus on one of the ideas, and members were asked to go back to their departments and come up with next steps. They scheduled a follow-up meeting to discuss these steps.

The discussion during the meeting was full of passion on both sides and because they had clear objectives to achieve, members were able to leave the meeting with a compromise and some innovative ways to improve the communication between the departments.

Groups are made up of different people, personalities, opinions, and goals. Debates are certainly not a bad thing during meetings because differing opinions and perspectives often lead to problem solving and "out-of-the-box" brainstorming. However, one of the most important roles for you as a Facilitator is to keep discussions on track, constructive, and respectful. As mentioned in the Teaming chapter, one way to do that is to set ground rules for the group at the first meeting and revisit them often. Start by posting basic rules like the ones below and then open it up for discussion to add to the list.

Common ground rules are:

- Be respectful of other group members and their ideas

- Avoid sidebar conversations

- Start and end on time

- Criticize ideas, not people

Stakeholders

Each meeting has a variety of stakeholders, and you need to make sure each stakeholder feels valued. One way to do that is through a "Check In" activity at the end of each meeting. While it might be difficult to do initially, the more comfortable group members become, the more honest they will be.

Check In's can start out as surveys sent to group members after a meeting. The surveys should ask what went well during the meeting, what could have gone better, and what members would like to see addressed in future meetings. As group members get more comfortable with each other, block off ten minutes at the end of each meeting to ask these questions. The answers will help keep the group on track and remind members that they have a say in the group's direction.

Group's Purpose

Some groups do not attain the goals they originally planned to achieve. A group may need to disband or shift its purpose because of other pressing priorities. Another common occurrence is that the group's purpose may have evolved over time so that the original goals and objectives are no longer applicable.

In any case, it's important to revisit the group's purpose and goals periodically to make sure that all group members are on the same page. There is nothing wrong in revising the group's goals but this must be done with the group as a whole so there is accountability and buy-in from everyone.

Managing Conflict

As a Facilitator, you need to know how to manage conflict so the group can continue to be productive and successful even when people disagree. When meetings become tense, here are a few tips to remember for managing anger:

- Maintain a non-anxious presence

- Assume the other person has good intentions

- Acknowledge the other person's feelings

- Lower your own voice

People have preferred styles of dealing with conflict, and, according to Thomas and Killman, there are **five conflict-management types: competition, collaboration, avoidance, accommodation,** and **compromise.** The style each person adopts depends on her level of assertiveness—how much she attempts to satisfy her own concerns—and her level of cooperation—how much she attempts to satisfy other's concerns.

Competition

The conflict-management style of competition is focused on power, putting one's own concerns and needs ahead of others'. While this may not be the best style for a Facilitator to have, as long as you are aware of the tendencies for this style, you can still be successful. This style can be helpful when decisions need to be made quickly such as in an emergency or near a deadline. However, if brainstorming is the goal, be cognizant of allowing discussion and debates to happen among the members.

Collaboration

Collaboration encourages discussion of different viewpoints, suggestions, and concerns. If this is your style, try to incorporate everyone's concerns and suggestions into the group decision so that everyone understands where each member is coming from.

Avoidance

The avoidance style works when a decision doesn't necessarily have to be made in a timely fashion. A Facilitator with this style needs to be aware that group members may become frustrated if you do not move the group toward a decision in a timely manner. However, this style could be helpful if tensions are high between different viewpoints and members need some time to cool down.

Accommodating

A Facilitator can use an accommodating style productively to get group members to come up with their own ideas and learn from their own mistakes. Often Facilitators have formed their own opinions or thoughts about a particular issue, but if you are truly a neutral party, having this type of conflict-management style will hold members accountable for their own decisions.

Compromising

A Facilitator with this middle-of-the-road style balances assertiveness and cooperativeness. This style works well if you have a looming deadline and need a quick solution to the problem. Keep in mind that to compromise, people have to give up something they want, so the chances the problem will come back to the table are highly probable.

Consensus

Getting to a group consensus can be challenging with different personality types in the group. However, it is important for the group to try to reach consensus decisions. Start off by asking if there were any ideas yet to be recorded. If not, start bringing attention to the ideas participants supported. This could be a vote or just a discussion.

If there are members who do not agree with the majority, say, "I see there are still some concerns about this idea. What do we need to discuss to address your concerns?" If after discussing concerns there is still no acceptance from a group member or two, then say "I know this is not your first choice, but can you live with the group's consensus of going with idea A?" Most people will be willing to go along with the group decision as long as it was recorded that they had a different idea or suggestion.

The FUN of Arbitrating is...

Seeing those group members who once were in a conflict or confrontation eventually work together and make progress on a project or idea.

Your FUNctional Attitude Focuses on:

- **Awareness** of the ever-changing dynamics within the group.

- **Patience** to arbitrate disputes as they occur.

T = TRAINING

This was an intact work team. The only new person on the team was the manager, and he knew his stuff. He had been doing this type of work for years and had achieved great success in his field. Now he was in a position of authority, managing a group of highly talented individuals who had been working without a manager for nine months. They were ready to be led. He was ready to lead.

The manager's plan was to facilitate this first meeting informally. He planned to use a round-table approach that would allow for equal give and take among the members. This was going to be a solid brainstorming session resulting in an appreciation of his laid-back, non-directive leadership style. He knew that facilitating a group was easy. He had seen it done many times before. All he had to do was introduce the topic and the group would take it from there. He was about to learn what it takes to be a good Facilitator.

Two hours later the group was in shambles. People were talking over each other. Some had disconnected from the group and were working on other projects. Some asked him to get involved in the discussion while others ignored him. The manager had no idea how to get the group under control. His inability to facilitate cost him the respect and cooperation of the one group of people he needed most in this new position, his team.

This manager thought facilitation was easy because the Facilitators he had seen had been trained in the art of facilitation and had made it look easy.

Facilitation is a learned skill. To do it right you need to know what to do, when to do it, and how to do it. After you have learned the what, when, and how, then you must practice. Each time you facilitate a group your skills are tested and you learn something new. Training to be a Facilitator requires continuous learning.

You can learn from a multitude of books (including this one, of course!) as well as articles in professional journals and magazines. There are also audio books, webinars, podcasts, and in-person seminars. Choose the method that best helps you learn.

The best learning comes from on-the-job training. Shadowing an experienced, successful Facilitator is a good way to start. Videotape a session and review it until you can pick out all of the intricacies of the Facilitator's technique. Then, and most importantly, adapt what you have read, heard, seen, and experienced to your own style. Great Facilitators are great because they are secure within themselves. They know their strengths and they know their limits.

When you research the various training programs that are available, look for programs that will develop your skills for working with adults, identifying and managing group dynamics, building consensus, and maintaining focus. Explore training programs that give you a variety of opportunities to practice facilitation skills and quality feedback on your performance.

The FUN part of Training is...

Learning something new every time you facilitate a group and applying that learning in your next facilitation.

Your FUNctional Attitude Focuses on:

- **Continuous learning** of different facilitation skills through workshops and webinars.

- **Observation** of other good Facilitators.

I = INTEGRATING

They were an intact work team responsible for supporting their customers. They were trained in the various products that their customers used, were provided with the most current updates for each product, and had access to other departments within the organization for any additional information they might need. They were customer focused. Each team member came to this department with a strong background in this type of product and in customer service. As individuals they were experts. As a team they were beginners.

Although each person knew his or her job they communicated poorly with each other. Cooperation and support within the group was non-existent. They had no knowledge of the company's goals or how their department fit into the bigger picture. As individuals they were disgruntled and dissatisfied and they were certainly not a team. The individuals were not happy, the customers were not satisfied, and the organization was not functioning as it should.

A Facilitator was hired to pull this team together. And quickly! The Facilitator first interviewed each person individually. The interview questions were designed to get baseline information on the processes each person used when interacting with customers.

> *More importantly, the interview was designed to build a relationship with the Facilitator. The Facilitator modeled open communication as she created an atmosphere of collaboration and trust between herself and individual group members. When the group came together the one relationship they all had was with the Facilitator. Now it was the Facilitator's job to integrate those individual relationships into group relationships that would form the group into a fully functioning team.*

Integrating diverse individuals into a team starts with building relationships among the individuals who make up that team. To do that you, the Facilitator, must model productive relationship and team behavior. That happens when you use active listening skills.

Listening actively is something most of us do not do. Ninety-three percent of all communication is non-verbal, and that includes the act of listening. Listening actively requires the listener to pay full attention to the speaker. The active listener **hears** the words and then concentrates on **understanding, interpreting**, and **evaluating** what he hears. Notice that all the bolded words are verbs (verbs describe actions – a short lesson in grammar here!). The active listener focuses on:

- **Maintaining eye contact** when the speaker is speaking.

- **Observing the speaker's posture**, looking for a comfortable, natural stance.

- **Vocalizing agreement** with "hmm" or "oh" or "ah."

- **Asking leading questions** to get more information i.e. "and then…?" or "what happened next?"

- **Paraphrasing** the speaker's words.

- **Using silence** to give the speaker time to think.

By using these skills during one-on-one interviews you will establish a relationship with each individual. Now build on those relationships and begin the integration process.

When you bring the group together use your knowledge of each person's strengths and weaknesses to guide group members to support each other. You can compliment the individuals and the group in general on the efforts they are making to complete their work. You will need to describe how their project fits into the overall goals of the company and the value they, as a team, are bringing to the organization. When they are aware of the skills they each bring to the team, encourage them to rely on each other for support as they move their project forward.

This integrating process for Facilitators is best summarized by Steven Covey: "Communication, after all, is not so much a matter of intellect as it is of trust and acceptance of others, of their ideas and feelings; acceptance of the fact that they're different and that, from their point of view, they are right."

The FUN part of integrating is...

Watching different attitudes and behaviors blend into one cohesive group.

Your FUNctional Attitude Focuses on:

- **Respect** of the group individually and collectively.

- **Responsiveness** to individual and group needs.

N = NOTETAKING

A group was recently assigned a new Facilitator and it was clear from her very first meeting that she didn't have much experience being in this position. She was disorganized, often sent the group the wrong meeting location, and forgot to follow up on tasks from meeting to meeting. She did not send out agendas or minutes prior to the meetings and at the beginning of each meeting she read every word of the minutes to the group.

As meetings continued like this, members' behavior started to shift. Some came late to the meetings because they knew the Facilitator would only be reading the minutes and they felt that she was being condescending by reading them. The Facilitator also got off track when reading the minutes because she would interject an update about a topic in the minutes instead of waiting to discuss it when it came up on the agenda.

Without an agenda to review before the meeting members weren't prepared to talk about specific topics, which only led to more wasted time during the meeting. If a member was supposed to have completed an assignment he or she often did not come prepared with an update because no one communicated between meetings. Membership started to dwindle because members felt that their time was being wasted.

Details of a meeting are very important because they help keep the members engaged and on track. For an effective group, a Facilitator needs to keep members up to date and informed of details. While there are different templates for agendas and minutes, they all include the same important details.

Agendas

Agendas are crucial because they tell members what to expect during the meeting. Agendas should go out a few days before the meeting so members can prepare if necessary.

An agenda should include, at a minimum, the following items to discuss during the meeting:

- Discussion topic

- Amount of time for each topic

- Who is responsible for presenting each topic

Some agendas also include a place for each member to record her own notes about discussions that occurred during the meetings. This often is helpful so that members can refer to their notes to make sure everyone came away from the meeting with the same information and messages. Here's an example of what a functional agenda might look like:

Discussion Topic	Amount of Time	Lead Person	Discussion/Action

Minutes

While a Facilitator has many roles, taking notes for the minutes is not one of them. The minutes of a meeting should be kept by a secretary, also called a scribe in some institutions. This person's role is to keep a record of discussions, assignments, and next steps.

Minutes should be sent out as soon as possible after the meeting so group members who missed the meeting know what was discussed. In addition, corrections can be made to the minutes if necessary because meeting details are fresh in everyone's mind. Sending out the minutes promptly also lets members who missed the meeting participate in the "next steps" agreed upon for each topic.

As mentioned in the above story, whether it's a week or a day before the next meeting, it's important to have the minutes sent out prior to the meeting so that time isn't taken away from the actual meeting by reading and looking over the minutes.

Newsprint

When a group is brainstorming ideas for a specific topic it's very helpful to use newsprint or a whiteboard to record all the ideas. This way everyone can see what ideas have already been expressed and shared.

Parking Lot Lists

A Parking Lot list refers to a white board or newsprint pad where you can maintain an ongoing list of questions or issues the group wishes to address. Parking Lot lists are a great way to record topics or ideas that come up, but are off the topic of the current discussion. This helps keep the discussion on track but also acknowledges group members' ideas and suggestions. Keep these ideas on visible newsprint so ideas can be added to the list throughout future meetings. Visible Parking Lot lists are also a constant reminder to go back to those topics.

Checking In

As discussed in the Framing and Arbitrating chapters, Check Ins are very important to the success of a group. While this isn't notetaking, Check Ins are important details that are often overlooked and can really help get a pulse on the members' motivation and satisfaction with the group as a whole. Facilitators should do a "Check In" at the end of the meeting to find out how everyone is feeling about the direction of the group's goal. This might feel a little uncomfortable at first, but the more you ask for "real-time" feedback, the more focused your group will be. Emailed or online surveys can also be used, especially if you're looking for specific suggestions on how to improve. Survey questions could include:

- Meeting length/pace? (poor, average, good, very good)

- Overall meeting effectiveness (poor, average, good, very good)

- What would you change to improve the effectiveness of the meetings?

The FUN of Notetaking is...

Keeping track of what goes on in the meeting so you can see all the accomplishments your group has made.

Your FUNctional Attitude Focuses on:

- **Organization** for required administrative tasks.

- **Management** of details for meetings and next steps.

G = GOOD GRIEF, THERE'S MORE!!

Over the years we have accumulated many hours of facilitation. We have facilitated in mediations of two to three people and we have facilitated small and large group workshops ranging from 5 – 50 people. Our groups have included intact teams, project teams, small units within larger departments, boards of directors, senior executive teams, and front line workers.

We have learned that, no matter the size, level of responsibility, or type of industry, all groups are both predictable and unique. Therein lies the FUN of facilitation. Just when you think you are prepared to facilitate the group in one direction, something, or often someone, changes the momentum.

What follows in this chapter are some situations we have experienced. Some of these situations may be familiar to you and some may be surprising. Some situations we handled well and some not so well.

We offer these situations to show you how we applied the techniques we've outlined in the previous chapters. Because **Firm, Fair, Focused,** and **FUN** facilitation requires you, the Facilitator, to incorporate your personalized approach into standard techniques, we challenge you to consider how you would handle these situations.

"No Guts, No Glory"

Part of the FUN of facilitating any group is the ever-present possibility of being surprised by what is said in the group. A Facilitator needs to be prepared to respond to those surprising statements casually and without judgments while keeping the group on track. This "no guts, no glory" story comes from a session in which the Facilitator used that phrase to encourage the group to speak their mind and to say what they needed to say without fear of reprisal. The Facilitator had used this phrase to motivate other groups to move forward in their process.

One of the individuals in the group had a very different interpretation of that phrase than did the Facilitator. She took the phrase very personally and reacted vehemently to its use. Her interpretation of "no guts, no glory" was one that the Facilitator had never encountered. In fact, the interpretation seemed completely illogical to the Facilitator.

Covering her surprise at the person's reaction and her own reaction to the lack of logic involved, the Facilitator immediately apologized for her use of the phrase. She explained that she was not aware of that interpretation and said that she could appreciate that people have different interpretations of different phrases. She stated firmly that she would not use that phrase again and thanked the individual for bringing a different interpretation to her attention.

Appreciating that everyone brings their own interpretation to every conversation is vital for a Facilitator. Bringing a non-judgmental attitude and valuing diversity is essential. Understanding that you will learn more from a group than you will ever teach will keep you alert in every session. It will also give you the satisfaction of knowing you have demonstrated the value you place on individual differences. The group will recognize that and your reputation as a quality Facilitator will be made.

The 80/20 Rule

The 80/20 rule is the more common name for the Pareto Principle. The Pareto Principle, the law of the vital few, states that 20% of your effort gives you 80% your return. Now let's apply this to the dynamics of a group. In any group there is a guarantee that 20% of the participants will be more negative or antagonistic toward the process than the remaining

80%. Another way to say this is 80% of your frustration will come from only 20% of the group.

Logic would tell you then that when or if the negative 20% leaves the group the remaining 80% will be positive and cooperate with the process. Ah yes, but human nature is fickle to say the least. Consider the concept that "nature abhors a vacuum." As soon as that 20% leaves the group the remaining 80%, to fill the vacuum, will splinter into a new negative, antagonistic 20%. And the pattern repeats.

Here's where your facilitation FUN begins. Since there is nothing you can do to prevent this from happening you need to be prepared to deal with that ever-present 20%. Don't be discouraged. It's not a bad thing. Preparing yourself for that 20% keeps you on your toes.

So, here's what you do. As we discussed in the Assessing chapter, prepare for each facilitation *before* the session by rehearsing every possible scenario in your head. With each scenario, practice the way you will handle the negative or antagonistic behaviors. Repeat that practice until your comfort level increases and you know that you will react calmly and appropriately in each situation.

Second, accept that people will always surprise you and every unexpected situation is a learning experience for you. You will learn more from that 20% than you will from the 80%. (The Pareto Principle in action: 20% of your experiences will give you 80% of your expertise as a Facilitator).

Third, find the FUN in the unexpected, turn the negative around, use the antagonism productively. Smile. Laugh. Enjoy your new-found knowledge.

The Dull Group

Let's not call them dull. Let's call them unmotivated or disinterested or bored or uncaring or, here's our favorite, forced to be in the group. No matter the label, this group is a challenge.

You are ready to work. You have prepped for days. You know the material. You have created an atmosphere that will foster progress. You have a plan.

They arrive late to the meeting. They forget their notes, their pens, their pre-work, their reason for being there. They put their cell phones on vibrate so they can take that one call they must answer today and, of course, they will have to leave the session when that call comes in. Although they are with you physically they are absent in every other sense. You take a breath.

You describe what you are seeing in the room. You ask if they are seeing the same thing. You ask them to describe the mood of the room. Then you stay silent as they talk, prompting them occasionally with a nod of your head or soft "ah" or "I see." The group may be silent for a long period of time. Some of you may have to practice becoming comfortable with silence. The quieter you are the more talkative they will be—honest!

Once they start telling you about their feelings, you may be hard pressed to turn them off. Allow them time to describe their feelings. When they are done or when you notice that they are winding down you ask them to stop. You summarize briefly. Then ask them what they want to do.

Remember this is your program so leaving is not an option and cancelling the program is not an option. Perhaps together, you could all revise the program to manage their concerns. Once they are involved in revising the program it becomes their program and you can move forward with your plan.

Now, here's the FUN part. Because you are a FUNctional Facilitator you knew you might encounter a group like this and in your original preparations for this program, you designed an alternate plan that is flexible enough to manage their concerns and fulfill your obligations to your client. An easy way to remember this is with the 5 P's: Proper Planning Prevents Poor Performance.

The Over Active Group

A group's Facilitator allows and invites the group to get off track from the agenda with off-topic stories. Many meetings go by without much progress because of these unfocused discussions. That's not to say that this group doesn't have passion, because it certainly does, and the agenda is always packed full of ideas and goals. However, with the lack of focus during the meetings, it's hard to accomplish those goals and members often leave asking, "Did we achieve anything?"

One way a FUNctional Facilitator could help keep this over active group on track is to assign a Timekeeper. Make sure the Timekeeper is someone who is not shy about interrupting a discussion and bringing the group's attention back to the agenda. Helpful phrases the Facilitator could use include "I'd like to take a minute and just bring the group back to the discussion at hand." Or, "I think we may have gotten a little bit off track. Can we put this topic on the Parking Lot list?"

The Leader-Less Group

It's hard for a group to succeed without an engaged leader. In this instance, the head of a department was recently promoted to his position and still related to the employees in his department as co-workers. When he led the monthly staff meetings it was clear he had few leadership skills. During the meeting the department head was more focused on his cell phone than the actual discussion that was happening around him. Discussions often got heated between employees because there was no Facilitator to guide them through constructive problem solving.

Employees often left these meetings more frustrated than when they came in, and they often went to management to complain about the lack of control the department head had. Eventually, management realized the department head's lack of leadership skills and provided him with additional training so he could be a FUNctional Facilitator and meet the needs of his department.

The Leader-Full Group

Some of the most fun you will have is facilitating a group of executives. In this group everyone is a leader in title and, many times, in ego. They all know the goal and they all have the solution.

What they may not have are effective active listening skills. Many people in leadership positions believe that they are leaders because they have all the answers all the time. (Actually, by definition, leaders are leaders because they have followers.) Bring a group of leaders together without followers and chaos can result.

So what do you do? First, appreciate that these people are used to power. You need to empower them in this group. Empower does not mean giving up control. It does mean that you become the leader of this group.

Second, give them control of their process by facilitating guidelines for their process. Have them create a contract for their communication and actions.

Third, hold them accountable to their contract. That means you need to be at the top of your game: strong, knowledgeable, and highly communicative. You need to be an effective, FUNctional Facilitator.

The Nonfunctioning Group

A Facilitator was asked to help with a group that was having difficulties achieving their goals. The meetings usually included a lot of yelling, heated discussions, and pointing of fingers. Initially, the Facilitator attempted to engage the group members by discussing ground rules, the goals, and purpose of the meeting. The discussion soon turned into chaos with people talking over each other.

The Facilitator attempted a different tactic, and asked for members to submit their feedback via email so that the introverted members had a voice too. He also reached out individually to members outside of the meeting, having honest conversations with them about the purpose of the group and why he needed their participation and involvement in the group. While the Facilitator tried to assign projects to different members within the group, he only received excuses and uncompleted assignments.

At the next meeting, the Facilitator had an honest conversation with the group to refocus and reiterate the goals and purpose of the group. There was much discussion among the members and in the end, it was decided that the group should disband as the interest had declined and work priorities had shifted. While this wasn't the original plan for the group, the Facilitator understood that priorities shifted and despite his best efforts, the group wasn't ready to tackle the goals they had originally set out for themselves.

Phrases to Facilitate Your Facilitation:

- "Hold that thought for a moment."

- "Let's stop here for just a minute and take inventory.... What are you all thinking right now?"

- "That's a great idea – let's discuss in a smaller group after this session."

- "If I could take a minute and just bring the group back to the discussion at hand."

- "I think we may have gotten a little bit off track. Can we put this topic on the Parking Lot list?"

- "What I'm hearing is that there is a concern about.... Is that correct? What can we do to address those concerns?"

Some Resources You Might Find Helpful:

One more thing...to be a FUNctional Facilitator you need to function as a Facilitator. That requires you to use your skills consistently and to learn continuously. What follows is a list of some of the resources we rely on to hone our skills. We encourage you to be on the lookout for new resources and to share them with other Facilitators. We know that knowledge and skills increase exponentially when we share them.

Covey, Stephen. *Principle Centered Leadership*, 1991. Simon & Schuster.

- Offers clear methods for self-development and building relationships with individuals and groups

Lencioni, Patrick. *Overcoming the Five Dysfunctions of a Team*. 2005. Jossey-Bass.

- Good insights into generalized team behavior with appropriate exercises that facilitate team development

Priest, Gass, and Gillis. *The Essential Elements of Facilitation*. 2000. Kendall /Hunt Publishing Co.

- A practical guide to facilitating organizational change based on corporate adventure programs

- An excellent follow up to FUNctional Facilitating

Schoel, Prouty, and Radcliffe. *Islands of Healing, A Guide to Adventure Based Counseling*. 1988. Project Adventure.

- Excellent resource for designing behavioral contracts that facilitate high-level group functioning

Schulte, Tom. "Facilitating Skills: The Art of Helping Teams Succeed". *Hospital Materiel Quarterly*: August 1999: 21, 1; AB/Inform Global p13.

- Helpful information on the basics of being a Facilitator: characteristics of a Facilitator, preparing for meetings, and making meetings productive

- Ways of handling conflict with a group

Thomas, K.W., and R.H. Kilmann. *Thomas-Kilmann Conflict Mode Instrument*. 1974. Xicom, Inc.

- Effective exercise to determine your style of handling conflict and ways to be successful with your style

CPP www.cpp.com

- Complete information on purchasing and scoring multiple assessments including the Myers Briggs Type Indicator

Survey Monkey www.surveymonkey.com

- Easy to use (and free) website to create online surveys to send to group members for evaluating effectiveness of meetings

Afterword

So there you have it - twelve techniques for facilitating your facilitation.

We have given you the basics. Now it is up to you to sift through the information, choose what you can use, file what you might need for later, and search for more.

A colleague of ours facilitates groups without labeling herself as a Facilitator. When we asked her which process or technique she used, she answered, "I just ask the right questions." She makes it seem so simple. We hope that the techniques we've shared in this book will make it simple for you.

We offer workshops on **The FUNctional Facilitator** where you will practice adjusting your attitude to be **Firm, Focused, And Fair**. To keep it simple, we design these workshops specifically for you and your organization. We follow the guidelines you've read about here, plus many more.

Because we know that all of us together are smarter than any one of us alone and that there is always more to learn, we look forward to hearing about your experiences in facilitation. Feel free to contact us at www.jtaylorconsulting.com.